21st CENTURY LIVES
SUPERMODELS

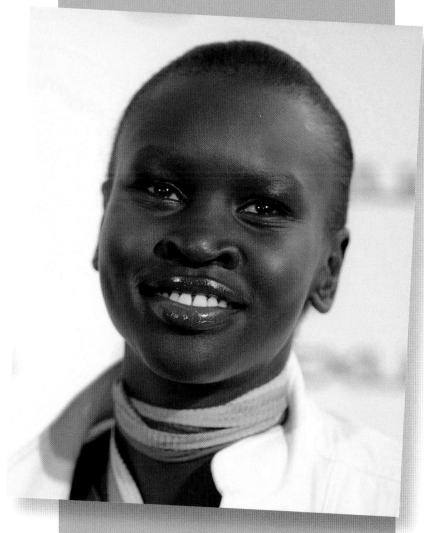

Liz Gogerly

WAYLAND

First published in 2008 by Wayland

Copyright © Wayland 2008

Wayland Books
338 Euston Road
London NW1 3BH

Wayland Australia
Level 17/207 Kent Street
Sydney NSW 2000

The right of Liz Gogerly to be identified as the author of the work has been asserted by her in accordance with the Copyright, Designs and Patents Act 1988.

Editor: Claire Shanahan
Designer: Fiona Grant
Design: Peter Bailey for Proof Books
Cover Design: Hodder Children's Books

British Library Cataloguing in Publication Data
 Gogerly, Liz
    Supermodels. - (21st Century Lives)
    1. Models (Persons) - Biography - Juvenile literature
    I. Title
    746.9'2'0922

ISBN 978 0 7502 5243 0

Cover: Supermodel Gisele Bündchen gets ready backstage at a Victoria's Secret fashion show in New York.
Evan Agostini/Getty Images: 20; Peter Andrews/Corbis: 9; Dave M Benett/Getty Images: 21; Vince Bucci/Getty Images: 16; Justin Canning/CBS/Getty Images: 7; Daniel Deme/epa/Corbis: 13; Matt Dunham/Reuters/Corbis: 18; Rune Hellestad/Corbis: 6; Peter Kramer/Getty Images: 14; Luke Macgregor/Reuters/Corbis: 8; Chris Moore/Catwalking/Getty Images: 19; Charles Platiau/Reuters/Corbis: 11; Reuters/Corbis: 5; Sebastian D'Souza/AFP/Getty Images: 15; Shannon Stapleton/Reuters/Corbis: front cover, 4, 17; Andrew H Walker/Getty Images: 12; Andrzej Wiktor/epa/Corbis: title page, 10.
Every attempt has been made to clear copyright. Should there be any inadvertent omission please apply to the publisher for rectification.

Printed in China

Wayland is a division of Hachette Children's Books, an Hachette Livre UK company.

Contents

Gisele Bündchen
The Brazilian bombshell

Gisele backstage at a Victoria's Secret fashion show in New York.

> **I was somebody who was 14 years old and who got an opportunity to do a job where I could make money, and, most important, to go to school and to help my family financially. And luckily I was successful in my job, thank God.**

Gisele Bündchen
http://www.celebsquotes.com

Name: Gisele Caroline Nonnenmacher Bündchen

Date of birth: 20 July 1980

Place of birth: Rio Grande do Sul, Brazil

Background: Looked set for a career as a professional volleyball player until a New York modelling agent spotted her when she was 14.

The look: Leggy and sexy. Gisele measures a whopping 1.8 metres (5 feet 11 inches) tall and has plenty of feminine curves.

Famous for: Starring on three covers in a row of the internationally acclaimed fashion magazine *Vogue*. Gisele was covergirl for November and December 1999 and January 2000. Since then she's fronted campaigns for top designer labels including Christian Dior, Dolce & Gabbana, Chloé, Louis Vuitton and Valentino.

High moment: Becoming the new face of the Red American Express card in 2006. Gisele is proud to be part of a campaign that helps people suffering from AIDS, tuberculosis and malaria in Africa.

Low moment: The 2004 film *Taxi*, in which Gisele starred with Queen Latifah, was a box office flop.

'X' factor: She's sexy and sensual, but she's also sporty and earthy.

Something you might not know about her: Gisele is into body adornment – she has a tattoo of a blue star on her wrist and her belly button is pierced.

Gisele Bündchen is reported to be the richest supermodel in the world. She rose to fame at the end of 1990s when the waif-look for models was 'in'. When Gisele hit the catwalks, with her long legs and womanly figure, she kick-started a new trend for curves. Her shapeliness has earned her the name 'The Body from Brazil'.

Gisele was born in 1980 in the small Brazilian town of Horizontina. She has a twin sister called Patricia and four other sisters. They all share Gisele's towering height and long, wavy, brown hair. At school, Gisele was teased for being so tall, but she turned her height to advantage on the volleyball court. At one time, she considered turning professional and playing for Sogipa, a Brazilian team. At 13, Gisele and her sisters took a course in modelling. It was during a trip to Sao Paulo with the modelling school that Gisele was spotted by Elite, one of the most famous modelling agencies. At the crucial moment of discovery, the story goes, Gisele was tucking into a McDonald's burger!

At 16, Gisele made her debut in New York at Fashion Week. At the time, she shared an apartment with six other models and her English was not very good. She quickly picked up the language and made a name for herself, with some of the top design houses signing her up for advertising work. In 1999, she made her debut on the cover of *Vogue*. The magazine believed Gisele had what it took to front a new look and ran an editorial with the headline, 'The Return of the Curve'.

Gisele has not looked back. These days she can take her pick of work assignments. She tries not to take the business too seriously and is reputed to be great to work with. When work's up, she likes nothing better than being at the beach or back on the volleyball court. She's had a string of high profile romances, most notably an on-and-off affair with Hollywood actor Leonardo DiCaprio. In 2004, she made her own film debut as a bikini-clad thief in *Taxi*. She was back on the big screen in 2006 in *The Devil Wears Prada*. In 2001 Gisele even launched her own line of footwear in Brazil. The company, called Ipanema, has sold over $100 million dollars of product since it began. With some of the profits going to charity, Gisele is shaping up to be a more than just a supermodel, she's a shrewd business woman and a philanthropist.

Gisele during filming of an advertisement in her native Brazil.

"Gisele was fabulous to work with. She was really into what we were doing. She wanted to experiment with a new look, which a lot of top models won't do. She's usually pictured looking glossy and glam, so we made her more edgy. It's that willingness to surprise people that keeps her at the top of her game."

Sophia Neophitou-Apostolou, Fashion Director of *The Sunday Times*, November 2003

weblinks

For more information about Gisele Bündchen, go to
www.waylinks.co.uk/ 21CentLives/Supermodels

Twiggy
The 60's Icon

Twiggy remains one of fashion's most famous faces. Since the 1960s, she's also become a well-known actress and television personality.

> **What happened to me in the Sixties was so major and so worldwide and so huge... But in a way, I had nothing to do with it, it just took me over... I was very, very underdeveloped for my age. I hated what I looked like, so I thought everyone had gone stark raving mad.**
>
> **Twiggy**
> ***The Evening Standard*, March 2004**

Name: Lesley Hornby (Twiggy is a nickname)

Date of birth: 19 September 1949

Place of birth: London, England

Background: Twiggy never dreamed of becoming an internationally famous model. At 16, she was spotted working as a hairdresser's assistant. Less than a year later, Twiggy became the face of London fashion. Her career took off in Paris, then America.

The look: Before Twiggy models tended to be older and more sophisticated. At 16, Twiggy was a mere 41 kilograms (6 stone). She was nicknamed 'Twiggy' because her legs were so thin.

Famous for: In October 1967, Twiggy made her first appearance on the cover of *Vogue*. Her short hair, spiky lashes and impish smile set her apart from other models of the day. The London-based designer Mary Quant created the mini skirt in the 1960s, which Twiggy wore and popularised around the world.

High moment: After 40 years in the business, Twiggy can still wow the crowds. Since Twiggy's appearance in the Marks and Spencer's advertising campaigns in the 2000s, sales in the shop have risen by more than 30 per cent.

Low moment: Television presenting. She left after just two months on the ITV show *Good Morning*. Her interviewing technique was criticised for being too wooden.

'X' factor: People trust and like her because she comes across as down-to-earth. Many women identify with her and believe they can look like her.

Something you might not know about her: In 1967, the Barbie company Mattel created a Twiggy doll. It was the first doll based on a supermodel. Naomi Campbell also has a doll made after her.

Twiggy stands in front of a photograpgh of herself as a teenager for America's Next Top Model.

Twiggy is often billed as the world's first supermodel. She rose to fame in the 1960s when *The Daily Express* proclaimed she was 'the face of '66'. This was the year that England won the football World Cup, Beatlemania gripped the world and London was swinging like never before. Doe-eyed, long and thin-limbed, Twiggy was another English export. She became a fashion icon everywhere and paved the way for more youthful and unusual looking models.

Lesley Hornby was the daughter of carpenter William Norman and shop girl Helen Hornby. They lived a comfortable working-class life in the north London suburb of Neasden. William hailed from Lancashire and many of his no-nonsense ways rubbed off on his youngest daughter Lesley. While she was shampooing hair at the salon where she worked, she had no idea that she would soon be swooped into the world of fashion and become its leading light. It was a young man called Justin de Villeneuve who saw her potential. He signed her to a modelling agency, became her boyfriend and suggested the short, chunky hairstyle that transformed her look. She changed her name to Twiggy and her modelling career took off.

Twiggy became an overnight sensation. She had always hoped that one day she might become a fashion designer. Instead, she became one of Britain's most famous models of that era. Part of her appeal was she was like the girl next door. She had a Cockney accent and was a complete innocent. The fashions of the day, particularly the miniskirt, worked well on her slender frame. She stayed top of the game until she decided to 'retire' from modelling in 1970 at the age of 19. Though Twiggy is remembered for being part of the swinging Sixties scene, she actually lead a quiet life. She lived at home with her parents and preferred needlework to partying.

After modelling, Twiggy turned to acting. In 1971 she took a leading role in the film *The Boy Friend*. Her singing, dancing and acting impressed many people and she won two Golden Globe Awards. Since then, she has appeared on stage and television. More recently she has made a name for herself as one of the judges on the American television show *America's Next Top Model*. However, it is her return to modelling for M&S in 2005 that has proved that she still has what it takes to be a top supermodel.

"She has an extraordinary beauty – a beauty that would have been unnoticed ten years ago… And her natural advantages will keep her in the public affections for some time to come. These assets include a Cockney accent, a lack of sophistication and of conceit, a limited vocabulary and a very sweet nature."

Fashion book *The Sixties: A Decade In Fashion*

weblinks

For more information about Twiggy, go to
www.waylinks.co.uk/ 21CentLives/Supermodels

Erin O'Connor
The 'imperfect beauty'

Erin at London Fashion Week 2007.

> 66 My teenage years were ridiculous. I desperately wanted a boob job, I desperately wanted a nose job, I constantly had sore feet because I would wear shoes two sizes too small because I couldn't bear to buy my big shoes... It was only in my late teens and early twenties, when I started modelling, that I began to appreciate myself. 99
>
> **Erin O'Connor**
> **The Guardian, September 2006**

Name: Erin O'Connor

Date of birth: 9 February 1978

Place of birth: Walsall, England

Background: Erin was a schoolgirl when scouts from the London-based modelling agency Models One spotted her potential. After a slow start, Erin took the scissors to her long thick dark hair. Her new short style allowed her natural features to shine and Erin hit the big time.

The look: 'Freak chic' – Erin's striking features, especially her large nose (she jokingly calls herself 'the Nose'), pale skin and long angular limbs means she stands out in a crowd of classically beautiful models.

Famous for: Erin is in with the top designers. She regularly works for labels like Chanel, Prada Versace, Christian Dior and John Galliano. In the 2000s, she has raised her profile with high-street shoppers in the UK with appearances in the Marks and Spencer campaigns.

High moment: A television programme all about her. In 2003, she appeared in *This Model Life* for Channel 4. The fly-on-the-wall documentary allowed Erin to show off her modest nature.

Low moment: Her teen years. She was teased for her looks and was very shy.

'X' factor: She's a one-off – nobody else looks like Erin. Expensive clothes work especially well on her willowy frame.

Something you might not know about her: In 2001, Erin appeared on the Royal Mail's Fabulous Hats collection of stamps. It was the first time that the name of the living person on the stamp was revealed to the general public.

Erin poses with models Lizzy Jagger and Laura Bailey for a Marks and Spencer television advertisement.

In 1996, Erin was visiting the Clothes Show Live at Birmingham NEC. She sported a brace and looked awkward as she hid behind a curtain of thick dark hair. However, scouts for top agency Models One still invited her to London to sign a contract. Later that year, Erin was photographed by the inspirational fashion photographer Jeurgen Teller. The photographs appeared in hip fashion magazine i-D with an editorial that introduced the new 'freak chic' and idea of imperfect beauty.

Erin's unusual beauty was not an instant hit. Critics in America simply didn't get her look. However, her big break came with a campaign for Gucci. At last, the fashion industry woke up to her potential. Since then she has appeared in *Vogue*, *Elle* and *Harper's Bazaar* and is a firm favourite with the top designers.

In 2006, Erin hit the headlines for all the wrong reasons. The fashion industry was under attack for promoting skinny models. Many young girls were suffering from eating disorders as a result of trying to be as slim as some supermodels. Erin was singled out as a bad role model. This was a difficult time for Erin as she is a naturally thin person. She has never needed to starve herself to remain slender. Fortunately, with experience and success behind her, Erin is confident enough to handle the criticism. As a school girl she would have hid behind her hair, but now she stands proud. With homes in London and New York and a passion for her work, Erin O'Connor is finally in the place she wants to be.

Erin O'Connor has been called everything from freak to magnificent. Since she first hit the headlines in 1996, she has carved out a successful career as the perfect 'anti supermodel'.

Erin was born in Walsall, a small town in the West Midlands. Her father worked in a foundry and her mother was a nursery teacher. Erin was the second of three girls. While her sisters developed curves, Erin seemed to keep growing upwards. At school, she bore the brunt of cruel jokes about her height. She was called Morticia (the ghoulish character from the cult television programme *The Munsters*) and Witch Fingers. Whenever she looked in the mirror she despaired at the size of her nose. Erin took comfort in reading and practised hard at ballet dancing.

"She isn't only a model. She is quite art [*sic*]. She is like theatre. She is extraordinary inspiration [*sic*]. I should love to be with her every day."

Fashion designer Jean Paul Gaultier

weblinks

For more information about Erin O'Connor, go to
www.waylinks.co.uk/ 21CentLives/Supermodels

Alek Wek

African Beauty

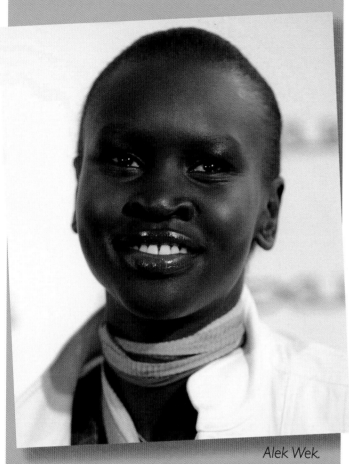

Alek Wek.

Name: Alek Wek (pronounced Uh Lek)

Date of birth: 16 April 1977

Place of birth: Sudan, Africa

Background: Alek was studying fashion technology and business at the London College of Fashion when a modelling scout spotted her. She was signed to London agency Models One in 1995.

The look: Alek has earned the name the 'face of Africa' because of her amazing ethnic look. Her full nose and lips and short black hair are a striking package that sets her apart from other more Anglo-looking black models.

Famous for: Alek caused a stir when she appeared on the November cover of American *Elle* in 1997. Readers were delighted that Alek's beauty was being celebrated. Since then Alek has been a favourite with designers such as Ralph Lauren, Christian Dior, Moschino and Issey Miyake and she has appeared on numerous magazine covers.

High moment: Scooping the MTV 'Model of the Year' and the *i-D* 'Model of the Decade' awards in 1997.

Low moment: Being parted from her family to move to London. It was two years before she saw her mother again.

'X' factor: A gift for positivity. When she's doing a fashion show she claims she always thinks how special and beautiful the clothes are because somebody's mother or sisters spent hours making them.

Something you might not know about her: Alek made her film debut in 2002 in *The Four Feathers* starring Heath Ledger and Kate Hudson. She played a Sudanese princess.

The African supermodel Alek Wek caused a sensation in the fashion world in 1997. Her look whipped up a debate about what is considered beautiful. Some people didn't appreciate her look, but for many she has become a fashion icon. Top fashion photographer Steven Meisel is just one admirer: "I haven't seen anybody that interesting, that black and that beautiful in a long time."

Alek Wek was born far away from the fashion catwalks of Europe and America. She is part of the Dinka tribe found in southern Sudan in Africa. Until she was 12, Alek lived in a small close-knit village of Wau with her parents and her eight brothers and sisters. They were all forced to flee to the capital city of Khartoum when civil war came to their area. In Khartoum, Alek's father died and the family had to make difficult decisions about its future. Alek moved to London to live with her sister in 1991. It worked out well for Alek who was quick to pick up English. She worked hard at school and made it to the famous London College of Fashion.

Alek was spotted by Models One when she was shopping at a street market in south London. Her major break came when she starred in singer Tina Turner's video for Golden Eye in 1995. Trendy magazines such as i-D and Frank featured her and the top fashion designers soon caught on. In 1996, she signed to New York-based agency Ford Models. She has since fronted campaigns for Clinique, Calvin Klein and Gap. Her look has opened up opportunities for other ethnic models. However, Alek does not want to be just seen as the 'face of Africa'. She refuses to go to castings for black models and will not wear typical 'African' gear such as leopard prints.

As well as making a name for herself as a top supermodel, Alek has turned her talents to bag design. In 2002, she launched a line of designer handbags, travel bags and briefcases called Wek 1933 Limited (after the year of her father's birth). Fashionable and functional, the bags have been a hit and production looks set for expansion in the future. Meanwhile, Alek has never forgotten her roots and the plight of her war-torn native country of Sudan. When she isn't modelling or designing bags, she is active on behalf of the US Committee for Refugee's Advisory Council. She visits schools and gives talks about the situation in southern Sudan today. She also works with AIDS,

The designer Karl Lagerfeld is a huge fan of Alek's beauty. He holds her hand at a Chanel fashion show in 2004.

children and breast cancer research charities. Her work and dedication to these causes shows how supermodels can make a difference in the world.

"I immediately thought of Alek Wek because she's an untypical model - again, someone who's broken a barrier, not the usual beauty you're used to seeing. She has incredible character, [she's] grounded, responsible, bright, and [has] a sense of humor… Alek is a symbol of optimism for the future."

Photographer Herb Ritts on why he chose Alek Wek to be the cover of the Pirelli calendar Women Through the Decade, http://www.herbritts.com

weblinks

For more information about Alek Wek, go to
www.waylinks.co.uk/ 21CentLives/Supermodels

Kate Moss
The Superwaif

Kate at an after-show party in New York in 2006. Kate is famous for enjoying a party lifestyle and is a regular at pop festivals and concerts.

" I'm uncomfortable with publicising myself... I can only say, over and over again, that's what I do, I'm a model. "

Kate Moss
The Face, 1996

Name: Katherine Ann Moss

Date of birth: 16 January 1974

Place of birth: London, England

Background: Kate was still a schoolgirl when Sarah Doukas, the founder of Storm Model Management, noticed her. The year was 1988 and Kate was at JFK Airport in New York on the way back from a holiday in the Bahamas. Her big break through came with a Calvin Klein perfume ad and a feature in *Vogue*.

The look: Less than perfect! Kate is just 1.68 metres (5 feet 6 inches) tall, which is short for a supermodel. She's also famously thin. Her best feature is her face with its high cheekbones and wide-set eyes.

Famous for: Kate has walked the catwalk and promoted products for most of the major labels and beauty companies. She's appeared on the cover of *Vogue* more than 20 times.

High moment: May 2007, when Kate launched a collection of her own designs for the high-street chain Topshop.

Low moment: In May 2006, Kate finally lost her temper with the paparazzi and kicked a photographer before stamping on his lens.

'X' factor: She's a free spirit with her own individual sense of style.

Something you might not know about her: Kate is rock 'n' roll through and through. She has appeared on music videos for The White Stripes, Elton John, Johnny Cash and Primal Scream.

Kate surprised on-lookers when she made a brief appearance in the window of the Topshop store on Oxford Street, London, the night before the launch of her first fashion collection.

starred in Calvin Klein's latest campaign. Soon afterwards the waif look caught on with Kate leading the way.

As well as being a high profile model, it is Kate's natural sense of style that has made her so popular. She has never hired a stylist and can be relied upon to invent new looks. Kate has been credited with making Ugg boots, welly boots, skinny jeans and waistcoats fashionable. The designer Marc Jacobs has even admitted to looking to Kate for inspiration for his new collections. In 2007, Kate's love affair with clothes led to her much anticipated collection for Topshop.

Kate has been called an icon of our times. Her famous face graces advertisements for Rimmel, Stella McCartney, Virgin Mobile, Christian Dior and Nikon. Even when she isn't working, the cameras are clicking. Fashion editors are keen to see what she's wearing and the gossip columns want to tell us all about what she's up to. In 2007, *Time* magazine placed her in The TIME 100, a list of people who shape our world. Love her or loath her, Kate Moss is one of the most successful supermodels of all time.

Katherine Ann Moss was born and raised in Croydon, South London. She was discovered at 14 and has been in the headlines pretty much ever since. Even so, much of Kate's life remains a mystery. This is because she rarely does interviews. Some people say this is because she is shy. Whatever the reason, this silence has fuelled the public's interest in her.

Kate's career kicked off with a series of black and white photographs in hip magazine *The Face* when she was 15. The supermodels of the day were commanding figures like Cindy Crawford and Naomi Campbell. In contrast, Kate was tiny and had an unusual beauty. Soon afterwards she appeared in a famous editorial in *Vogue*. Kate was photographed in a shabby flat wearing scanty underwear. Critics thought she looked seedy and underfed. However, designers such as Calvin Klein spotted her potential. In 1993, Kate became an international sensation when she

As well as clothes, Kate has a colourful personal life. She has dated screen idol Johnny Depp, James Bond actor Daniel Craig and in recent years the singer Pete Doherty. In between working and partying, she has also found time to become a mother. Her daughter Lila Grace was born in 2002, two years before Kate celebrated her 30th birthday. Next came the cocaine scandal that should have ended her career. However, Kate has bounced back to become even more successful, scooping major campaigns and earning more than ever. Like so much about Kate, it is a mystery why she remains at the forefront of fashion. She's at an age when most supermodel's careers have ended, yet Kate doesn't appear to be going anywhere…

"She is one of the few women alive today who I think is a contemporary icon…"

Alexandra Shulman, the editor of *Vogue*, *The Telegraph*, August 2006

weblinks

For more information about Kate Moss, go to
www.waylinks.co.uk/ 21CentLives/Supermodels

Marcus Schenkenberg
First Male Supermodel

Over 15 years in the business and Marcus still looks like a top supermodel as he walks the runway for Johnnie Walkers Dressed to Kilt 2007 fashion show.

"Once you've worked with people you want to leave a good impression, so that people want to work with you again... always be professional. Stay healthy and strong, work out and eat healthy and have a good attitude."

Marcus Schenkenberg's tips for being a supermodel, www.modellaunch.com

Name: Marcus Lodewijk Schenkenberg van Mierop

Date of birth: 4 August 1968

Place of birth: Stockholm, Sweden

Background: Marcus headed to Los Angeles, USA, from Sweden when he was 17. In 1988, a photographer called Barry King spotted him rollerblading on Venice Beach. A few months later Marcus was in Paris working as a model. The Calvin Klein campaign in which he starred in 1991 made him the most sought-after male model in the world.

The look: With his sculptured features, washboard stomach muscles and well-honed body, Marcus is a like a walking Adonis.

Famous for: The shower scenes from the 1991 Calvin Klein campaign and the 1993 shots for Versace. Suddenly, women everywhere wanted to know who this drop-dead gorgeous man was, and men wanted to look like him.

High moment: Starring on a 1991 cover of *Harper's Bazaar*, becoming the first male model ever to appear on the cover of a fashion magazine.

Low moment: Marcus can speak five languages including English, Swedish, Dutch, Italian and French. Why then did he choose to record a song in Spanish called *La Chica Marita*? It was not a hit!

'X' factor: As well as being gorgeous, Marcus is reported to be a very funny, kind person who hasn't allowed success go to his head.

Something you might not know about him: In 1997, he wrote a book about his career and the fashion business called *Marcus Schenkenberg: New Rules*. The proceeds from the book were donated to Multiple Sclerosis charities because his brother Michael has the disease.

Marcus Schenkenberg has been called 'a cartoon fantasy man'. He is best known as the first male supermodel. His rippling muscles first caught our eyes in the 1990s at the height of the supermodel era. Many say he was the only man beautiful enough to be photographed alongside the most famous supermodels of the era, such as Claudia Schiffer, Naomi Campbell and Linda Evangelista.

Marcus poses in front of a billboard advertisement against illegal bird trading as part of his spokesperson role for PETA.

He was born in Stockholm, Sweden. The teenage Marcus was far removed from the statuesque vision of manliness we see today. He was lanky and shy but loved to play basketball. When he was 17, Marcus headed to Los Angeles, on the west coast of the USA, to see what life in the States could hold for him. First he got a job looking after five dogs, then he was a nanny for children. In his spare time, he was at the beach or practising rollerblading. In 1989, he was skating on Venice Beach wearing bright pink shorts and a pink bandana when photographer Bill King spotted him. Soon afterwards Marcus signed to the Boss modelling agency in New York. He chose them because they didn't seem to mind his long hair. Very soon, Marcus began a whole new trend for long hair for men.

1991 was the big year for Marcus. He took part in the famous Calvin Klein campaign photographed by Bruce Weber. Marcus posed nude in the shower. He was one of many other models Bruce photographed that day and Marcus had no idea he would become the main male face of the campaign. The same year, Marcus was on the cover of *Harper's Bazaar*. Since that memorable year, Marcus has appeared on many other magazine covers and he's modelled for most of the major labels, including Versace, Missoni, Christian Dior and Givenchy. He is credited by many in the fashion business as putting male modelling on the map.

You only have to look at Marcus to see the secret of his success. However, he is also reported to be laid-back, easy to work with and happy to take risks with his image. He even wore long body-hugging gowns, lacy gloves and make-up for a Jean Paul Gaultier show. And, for Alexander McQueen's opening show for Givenchy, he donned huge feather wings and a white loin cloth.

Marcus has also cultivated a career outside the fashion industry. He's written a book, released a record and starred in films and television programmes. He has homes in New York and Milan in Italy. In Italy he's a correspondent for *The Corlucci Cald Show*, in which he interviews players and reports on major soccer games. He also co-hosts a comedy variety show called *La Grande Note de Lunadi Sera*. As if this isn't enough, Marcus supports the charity PETA (People for the Ethical Treatment of Animals).

"After Marcus's first famous pictures, men everywhere grew their hair out like his, paid more attention to their bodies, and to how the clothes actually fit them. Men are taking a cue from Marcus and are feeling comfortable about expanding their self-expression, about being sexy and beautiful. And it's just the beginning..."

The late fashion designer Gianni Versace
http://marcusschenkenberg.org/

weblinks

For more information about Marcus Schenkenberg, go to
www.waylinks.co.uk/ 21CentLives/Supermodels

Tyra Banks
Swimsuit Sensation

The retired supermodel Tyra Banks still looks every bit a professional model as she arrives at a style awards ceremony in 2007.

> " Victoria's Secret said I sold more bras and panties than anybody else, and I was traipsing down that runway with 30 pounds more booty than the other girls. So it had to a lot to do with my success, my weight, but it's also been an issue for me, so I can relate. "
>
> **Tyra Banks**
> *The Guardian, April 2007*

Name: Tyra Lynne Banks

Date of birth: 4 December 1973

Place of birth: California, USA

Background: Tyra was set to start university when she was signed by top agency Elite. Her first assignment was in Paris. At the time, Tyra decided she would spend a couple of years modelling before returning to her studies. After Paris, her career rocketed and Tyra never went back to school.

The look: Sexy and curvaceous.

Famous for: In 1997, Tyra became the first Afro-American girl to appear on the cover of the famous American magazine *Sports Illustrated* wearing a bikini. She was also one of the most popular models for the top lingerie company Victoria's Secret.

High moment: Tyra is tipped to become the next Oprah Winfrey (the American chat show queen) with the success of her television daytime talk show *The Tyra Banks Show*.

Low moment: Being photographed looking 'fat' in a bikini on holiday in Australia in 2006. Headlines such as 'America's Next Top Waddle' and 'Tyra Porkchops' hurt the ex-supermodel's confidence.

'X' factor: Those curves – at the height of her career she was asked to lose weight, but the extra kilos probably added to her success.

Something you might not know about her: Tyra has a good singing voice and nearly released her own album called *T.Y.R.A.* However, her first single *Shake Ya Body*, released in 2004, didn't do well.

Tyra Banks is more than just a supermodel. At the height of her modelling days, she was acting, singing and hosting the television show *America's Next Top Model*. Since she quit the catwalk in 2005, she has hosted her own talk show *The Tyra Banks Show*. And now she's establishing herself as a spokesperson for women of every colour, shape and dress size.

Tyra wasn't always so confident and sure of herself. Her parents divorced when she was six. At school in Los Angeles, she was teased for being too tall and skinny. In desperation, she consumed peanut butter and chocolate milkshakes. One day she looked in the mirror and saw curves. However, when somebody told her she could be a model she still didn't believe it. She thought her eyes were too far apart, her chin was too narrow and her lips weren't wide enough. Four modelling agencies rejected her before Elite finally signed her when she 17.

Tyra went on to become one of the best-known models of the late 1990s. She has worked for major labels such as Ralph Lauren, Dolce & Gabbana, Chanel, Yves Saint Laurent and Tommy Hilfiger. She also appeared on numerous magazine covers including *Vogue*, *Harper's Bazaar*, *Elle* and *Sports Illustrated*. However, it was when she modelled lingerie for Victoria's Secret that people really began to celebrate her shapeliness. Tyra always claimed she didn't watch her weight. She ate what she wanted and kept in shape playing basketball and tennis. At the height of her career she was asked to lose weight by other companies, but when she worked for Victoria's Secret she was allowed to be herself – it's a message she now promotes to women everywhere.

The weight issue has followed Tyra into her media career. In 2006, she became the centre of a controversy about women's bodies. When an unflattering photograph of Tyra in a swimsuit appeared in an American tabloid, she decided to fight back. She appeared on her TV chat show wearing the same swimsuit. True she'd gained a few kilos, but she also looked sensational. Since then, Tyra has regularly spoken out against women being labelled as 'fat' or 'ugly'. On her show she's gone undercover as a fat person (using a fat suit) to see how heavier people are victims of discrimination. She's also braved a visit to a high security female prison to highlight the lives and experiences of different women. Such ventures have earned her respect and top television ratings.

Tyra became one of the most famous models for lingerie giant Victoria's Secret.

These days the ex-supermodel is perhaps better known as a role model. In 2007, she capped it all by being named as one of the top 100 most influential people in the world by *Time* magazine.

"She's one of the most hardworking people I know – I've seen her go straight from a late night of press to an early-morning shoot with no complaints. Even more important, she is passionate about her projects and compassionate toward the people involved in them. Her appeal is obvious to anyone who knows her, whether personally or professionally or just from her shows."

Fellow model Heidi Klum,
Time magazine, April 2006

weblinks

For more information about Tyra Banks, go to
www.waylinks.co.uk/ 21CentLives/Supermodels

Lily Cole
Living Doll

Lily scooped the model of the year award at the 2004 Fashion Awards in London.

> **When half the world is starving and a good proportion of the other half is suffering from obesity, to put me on the front page is ridiculous. I'm fine. I'm healthy. I eat.**
>
> Lily Cole speaks out against the tabloids that blame her for the trend for skinny models,
> *The Telegraph,* September 2006

Name: Lily Cole

Date of birth: 19 May 1988

Place of birth: Torbay, England

Background: Lily was a 14-year-old schoolgirl when she was spotted by a scout from the Storm modelling agency. At the time, Lily was more interested in her studies than becoming a supermodel. However, after a photo shoot for Italian *Vogue* in 2003, Lily became one of the most exciting new faces of fashion. Many people tipped her to become the 'next Kate Moss'.

The look: With her flame red hair, porcelain complexion and doll-like features, there is no mistaking Lily for anyone else. She has been described as looking like a Pre-Raphaelite maiden.

Famous for: Lily's unusual features have graced campaigns for Prada, Hermes, Chanel, Cacherel, Top Shop, Accessorize, Alexander McQueen, Moschino's I Love Love perfume and Ghost's Anticipation perfume.

High moment: Being voted 'Model of the Year' at the 2004 British Fashion Awards.

Low moment: Lily turned a potential low moment into a high one by ending her contract with the diamond company De Beers, as soon as she heard that it had been involved in the removal of native bushmen from their land in Botswana.

'X' factor: She's more than just a pretty face. In 2007, Lily started a degree in social and political sciences at Cambridge University.

Something you might not know about her: Lily is a member of the charity Trees for Cities because she believes trees are important in urban areas. She also supports the charity Environmental Justice Foundation that campaigns to stop forced child labour within the cotton industry.

Lily's striking looks lend themselves to out-of-this-world fashions. In 2007, she wowed the crowds at the Jean-Paul Gautier fashion show with his unusual creation.

British teenage supermodel Lily Cole is leading a new trend for ethereal, unusual looking models. Elfin models Gemma Ward, Devon Aoki and Heather Marks follow in her wake. Though it's Lily's stunning red hair that turns people's heads, it's her mind that makes her stand out in her profession.

Lily was born in Brixham, a seaside town in south Devon. She was five when her father, a fisherman, and her mother, an artist, divorced. Lily moved with her mother to London where she showed signs of being a good student. Her teenage ambition was to get to Cambridge University. At 14, Lily was spotted in Soho in London by a scout from the agency Storm Models. At the time, Lily was munching a hamburger! She ran away when this 'dodgy guy' started to talk to her. Her friends had to persuade her to listen to what the man had to say.

Fortunately, Lily did stop and listen and ultimately signed to Storm. Less than a year later, in 2003, she was photographed by top photographer Steven Meisel for *Vogue*. Lily's striking looks were an instant success. Her modelling career took off with covers for *Vogue* and *Numero*. *Vogue's* editor Alexandra Shulman is amazed by her 'utterly compelling' looks and has placed her on the cover four times. By 18, Lily had become the face of top fashion labels such as Prada, Hermès and Moschino. She'd already walked the catwalks for giants like Chanel, Louis Vuitton, Christian Lacroix and Alexander McQueen.

Lily is a popular, hard-working model, but behind the scenes she's also a determined scholar. Throughout her career she's always claimed that her school work came first. In 2005, Lily passed four A-levels with top grades in all her subjects. She scooped school prizes and earned a place at King's College, Cambridge.

The year 2007 was busy for Lily. Early in the year, she began working on her first feature film. She joined the cast of *St Trinian's*, a re-make of a famous British comedy set in a girls school from the 1950s. Lily plays Polly, a schoolgirl swot with pigtails and spectacles. Then, in September 2007, Lily finally began a degree at Cambridge University. For now, her fashion career is on hold, but people in the business don't think that we've seen the last of Miss Cole.

> "Lily is really unique and it is all about finding a truly special face. She has this china-white perfection, a delicate doll-like look, with her flame red hair set against that porcelain skin, which makes her the perfect model for the ultra feminine designs that have filled the catwalks in the last few seasons. She has a great work ethic and clearly loves being part of the fashioin industry."
>
> Elizabeth Norris, bookings editor of *Harper's Bazaar, The Daily Express*, March 2007

weblinks

For more information about Lily Cole, go to
**www.waylinks.co.uk/
21CentLives/Supermodels**

Jamie Dornan
The Singing Supermodel

Singing and acting are in Jamie's blood. He attended the New York premiere of the Hollywood film Marie Antoinette, *in which he co-starred with Kirsten Dunst.*

"The reason [modelling has] worked so well for me is that I don't take it all too seriously... It's a great business for now, a great way to make money and have a laugh... Who knows what's next?"

Jamie Dornan
International Herald Tribute,
November 2006

Name: Jamie Dornan

Date of birth: 1982

Place of birth: Belfast, Northern Ireland

Background: Jamie was always more interested in acting and rugby than modelling. He was signed to modelling agency Select after appearing on the Channel 4 television show *Model Behaviour.* Next came major campaigns for Dolce & Gabbana and Christian Dior. Now he's recognised as one of the top male supermodels of the moment.

The look: A bit of a pretty boy. Jamie's clean-cut and athletic, and likes to keep in shape playing rugby.

Famous for: He's the face of Dior Homme, the famous fragrance for men. In 2007, he appeared alongside Gisele Bundchen in a global advertisement for Aquascutum.

High moment: The photo shoot for Asprey on which he met the Hollywood actress Keira Knightley. They dated for two years, becoming one of the most talked about celebrity couples. This did a lot to boost Jamie's modelling career.

Low moment: Writing *Only on the Outside.* The song is about a couple splitting up, but Jamie denies that it is about the end of his relationship with Keira Knightley.

'X' factor: "Everyone loves an Irish boy!" Jamie's not just good looking – he has plenty of Irish charm.

Something you might not know about him: Acting is in his blood. He's the great grandson of the famous 1940s British actress Greer Garson.

Jamie with the actor James Purefoy at a London charity event in 2007.

The Northern Irish model Jamie Dornan is proving more than just a pretty face. He's a singer songwriter for the band Sons of Jim. And, in 2006, his Hollywood debut in the glossy film *Marie Antoinette* really got the critics talking…

Jamie Dornan was born in Belfast in 1982. His father, Jim Dornan, grew up with dreams of becoming an actor. Instead he studied medicine and became one of Northern Ireland's leading obstetricians (specialists in childbirth). Jamie's mother died when he was a teenager and he spent much of his childhood growing up in Holywood, County Down. His father's interest in acting rubbed off on him and he joined a local theatre group with which he even toured for a while. He went to Belfast Methodist School and left with three A-levels in English, Classics and History of Art. His main interest at school was rugby. After school, he joined the Harlequins rugby club in Belfast and looked set to go to university.

In 2001, Jamie's older sister Jessica told him about an advertisement in the local paper for a Channel 4 programme to find new models. Jamie turned up at the auditions with a friend for a laugh. He didn't expect to be chosen for the show, yet *Model Behaviour* turned out to be his springboard to success. He didn't win the show, but he was signed to Select modelling agency soon afterwards. He started off doing work for the pre-teen magazine market, but it wasn't long before he caught the eye of top photographers, leading labels and fashion editors. Campaigns for Christian Dior and Dolce & Gabbana secured his name. More recently, he's partnered Kate Moss for a classy Calvin Klein campaign.

Jamie's music career has been quietly bubbling away in the background while his modelling takes centre stage. For many years he's been singing and writing songs with David Alexander, a friend from his school days. The duo have formed the folk-pop band Sons of Jim (named after their fathers who both happen to be called Jim) and set up their own record label, Doorstep. They've toured with KT Tunstall and released a single. In 2007, major labels were beginning to show an interest in the band and they are recording their first album.

As well as singing, Jamie has added film acting to his CV. Top Hollywood director Sofia Coppola chose him to play a dashing Swedish count in the 2006 movie *Marie Antoinette*. Jamie got many favourable

reviews for his small part. These days Jamie is not sure quite where his career will take him next. But for now he's enjoying himself: "I just love the attention!" he says, "I don't really mind where it comes from."

"He's like the male Kate Moss. His proportions are a little off. He has a slight build. He's on the small side for male models. But his torso is long, and so he looks taller, and he brings a relaxed quality to modelling. He knows what he's there for, but unlike a lot of people he's not trying to be a male model."

Jim Moore, creative director of *GQ* magazine, *International Herald Tribune*, November 2006

weblinks

For more information about Jamie Dornan, go to
www.waylinks.co.uk/ 21CentLives/Supermodels

Other Supermodels

Laetitia Casta

The French supermdoel Laetitia Casta was born in Normandy on 11 May 1978. She's best known for her amazing curves, which turned her into one of the top models for lingerie giant Victoria's Secret. She also starred on the cover of *Sports Illustrated* swimsuit edition three times in a row. Since her career began in 1993, she has appeared on over 100 magazine covers including *Elle* and *Vogue*.

Laetitia was spotted by the Parisian agency Madison Models when she was just 15. At the time, she was digging sandcastles on the beach and her father had to be persuaded to let his daughter be photographed. She went on to become the model for Yves Saint Laurent, Chanel, L'Oreal and Christian Dior. In 1999, she was chosen to become the new model for the bust of Marianne. This is a great honour in France because Marianne is a symbol of the French Republic and a bust is found outside each French town hall. The same year, Laetitia made her debut in a film called *Astérix et Obélix contre César* (1999). Laetitia has two young children and lives in London. These days, she combines her modelling career with acting in mainly French language films.

Sophie Dahl

Sophie Dahl is the granddaughter of the children's author Roald Dahl. She was the inspiration for his character Sophie in the book *The BFG*. She's gone on to become an author herself. However, when Sophie burst onto the modelling scene when she was just 18, she was famous for being large and lovely.

The British supermodel was born in London on 15 September 1977. Her mother Tessa Dahl is also an author and her father Julian Holloway is an actor. Sophie was discovered crying on her front doorstep after an argument with her mother by the flamboyant fashion editor of *Vogue*, Isabella Blow. At the time Sophie didn't fit the usual supermodel mould because she was a size 16. But her beautiful doll-like features and her ample curves soon got her noticed and she became a favourite model for top designers including Karl Lagerfeld. One of her most memorable campaigns was the nude black and white advertisements for the Yves Saint Laurent perfume Opium. Unfortunately, the British general public found the posters too shocking and they were eventually banned.

More recently, Sophie has slimmed down and settled down to write. In 2003, her first novella, a romantic fairytale called *The Man with the Dancing Eyes*, was released. The same year she became the new face of the Scottish knitwear company Pringle.

Tyson Beckford

The American supermodel Tyson Beckford reckons that if he hadn't become a model he'd be living a life of crime. Once upon a time this strapping supermodel was a member of New York street gangs. These days he is the leading man for designer Ralph Lauren and one of the highest paid male models in the world.

Tyson was born in New York on 19 December 1971. His striking features are down to his Jamaican father and his Chinese-American mother. He was raised in New York and Jamaica. After high school, he became involved with street gangs that were violent and dangerous. His life was going nowhere when, in 1991, a chance discovery by the editor of the hip-hop magazine *The Source* put him on the road to success. He signed to a New York agency and in 1993 was snapped up in an exclusive contract by Ralph Lauren. Before long,

Tyson was featured in magazines such as *Vogue* and *GQ*. These days, he combines modelling with acting. As well as music videos (he's in Britney Spear's *Toxic*), he's appeared in *Zoolander* (2001), *Gas* (2004) and *Hotel California* (2008).

Natalia Vodianova

The Russian supermodel Natalia Vodianova is often called 'Supernova'. By the age of 21, she was married to a member of the British aristocracy and had two children. She'd also landed work for Louis Vuitton, L'Oreal, Calvin Klein and Gucci.

Natalia is a classic Cinderella. She was born on 28 February 1982 in the Russian city of Gorky (now Nizhny Novgorod). She was raised by her mother, and had a poor childhood. When she was 15, Natalia left home and set up a market stall selling vegetables. It was here that she was spotted by a scout from Paris. She was told that she could be a massive success if she learned English in three months. Natalia was desperate to help her family. By 17, she'd learned English and moved to Paris. Gucci signed her to market its new perfume and she also worked for Calvin Klein. Then, at 19, on the brink of making it big, she met and fell in love with Justin Portman, the British heir to a rich real estate business. Within two years, she was married with a son and daughter. However, being a wife and mother has not stopped the blue-eyed, dark blonde supermodel in her tracks. She is one of the top supermodels of the moment. She's appeared on the covers of *Vogue* and *Vanity Fair* and her mammoth list of clients include Vivienne Westwood, Christian Dior and MaxMara. She lives in New York and is expecting her third baby.

Aishwarya Rai

The actress and model Aishwarya Rai is often called the queen of Bollywood. She's also an ex-Miss World who shot to fame after appearing in a Pepsi advertisement.

Aishwarya was born on 1 November 1973 in Mangalore in southern India. The family moved to Bombay (now Mumbai) when she was four. She was studying architecture at the university in Mumbai when her modelling career took off. Her perfect features and stunning blue-green eyes brought her contracts with Pepsi and Palmolive. She caught the attention of top photographer Steven Meisel who photographed her for *Vogue*. She carried on with her studies until 1994 when she scooped the Miss World title. After three years of working on Indian fashion magazines, Aishwarya turned her talents to acting. Her first commercial success was the Tamil-language film *Jeans* (1998). However, she is most famous for the films she has made in Bollywood including *Taal* (1999) and *Devdas* (2002). In 2004 she made her first English-speaking film, *Bride and Prejudice*. Though Aishwarya's modelling days seem to be mainly behind her, she is still considered to be one of the most beautiful women in the world. In 2000, she was voted the Most Beautiful Miss World of All Times and in 2003 she graced the cover of *Time* magazine.

The History of the Supermodel

The term 'supermodel' applies to a model who regularly works for the major fashion labels and appears on the covers of top fashion magazines such as *Vogue* and *Harper's Bazaar*. The word 'supermodel' was first used to describe models such as Twiggy, Jean Shrimpton and Veruschka in the 1960s. However, in the 1980s models took on a new celebrity and earned more money than before. The 'trinity' of supermodels was Christy Turlington, Linda Evangelista and Naomi Campbell. Evangelista once famously said, "I don't get out of bed for less than $10,000 a day." Other leading lights of the 1980s and 1990s were Cindy Crawford, Claudia Schiffer, Elle McPherson and Kate Moss. By the 2000s, the era of the supermodel was supposed to be over. These days film actresses and famous celebrities are as likely to lead advertising campaigns as models. However, the term 'supermodel' is still used to describe those models who are successful and have that extra special quality that sets them apart from the rest.

Index